YOU HEAR ME?

poems and writing by teenage boys

YOU HEAR ME?

poems and writing by teenage boys

edited by Betsy Franco

CANDLEWICK PRESS

First paperback edition 2001

The Library of Congress has cataloged the hardcover edition as follows:

You hear me? : poems and writing by teenage boys / edited by Betsy Franco.
— 1st ed.
p.   cm.
Summary: An anthology of stories, poems, and essays by adolescent boys on
issues that concern them.
ISBN 978-0-7636-1158-3 (hardcover)
1. Adolescence — Literary collections. 2. Youths' writings.
[1. Adolescence — Literary collections. 2. Youths' writings.]   I. Franco, Betsy.
PZ5. F925 2000
810.8'092836 — dc21   99-057129

ISBN 978-0-7636-1159-0 (paperback)

12 13 14 15 16 17 BVG 16 15 14 13 12 11

Printed in Berryville, VA, U.S.A.

This book was typeset in Officina.

Candlewick Press
99 Dover Street
Somerville, Massachusetts 02144

visit us at www.candlewick.com

For my sons, James, Thomas, and David

CONTENTS

PREFACE

P eople warned me that if I wanted to compile an anthology of stories and poems by teenage boys, I wouldn't receive any submissions. But in the summer of 1998, I felt compelled to launch the project *You Hear Me?* anyway. After all, I had three sons of my own, and I knew how important it was to hear from boys. Also, my experience compiling *Things I Have to Tell You,* a collection of writing by teenage girls, had taught me that it was worth the risk.

The focus and significance of *You Hear Me?* didn't become clear until I had received several dozen submissions and had spoken to a number of the authors. It became apparent that boys needed a forum to speak for themselves on issues that concerned them. One author was very relieved to hear that I wasn't going to be including commentary to clarify the work, or as evidence of a theory. He said he'd read a number of books in high school that supposedly addressed boys' issues . . . and he "couldn't relate."

My philosophy has been that people should speak for themselves. In the case of teenage boys, I've noticed that people tend to put words and feelings into boys' mouths, based on secondhand information and stereotypes. In *You Hear Me?* I wanted to present the uncensored accounts of teenage boys without the filter of adult sensibility.

In collecting the pieces, my goal was to include all kinds of voices—from the suburbs to the heart of the city, from those who love to write to those who just have something to say, if someone will listen. The collection includes stories, poems, and essays from across the country. I advertised in creative writing journals, found an Internet site that linked me to forty-eight hundred classrooms, collected poetry from writing projects in Detroit, Houston, and Chicago, and invited individual boys to submit.

As the collection grew, I noticed a frankness and honesty, but also a sensitivity in the writing. *You Hear Me?* shows the inner and the outer sides of boys. I knew from my own sons that boys have a broad emotional range, but I wasn't sure that they would be willing to share their thoughts and feelings in a publication. I found out that they are willing, and the result is a powerful statement of who they are.

Betsy Franco

ACKNOWLEDGMENTS

S o many people helped with this book. The first person I spoke to was Thomas Schellenberg, a gifted creative writing teacher, who let me talk to his classes at Palo Alto High School and helped me gather submissions for the book. Next I contacted Terry Blackhawk's InsideOut Writing Project, an outstanding program of poets in the Detroit schools. When she sent me her powerful selections, the book had a foundation. Throughout the project, Terry offered her advice, support, and enthusiasm. Poets-in-residence, teachers, and support staff connected to the InsideOut poets include John Aldrich, Therese Becker, Peggy Bodenmiller, Louis Carney, Dawn McDuffie, Helen Didley, Arbrie Griffin, Sheryl Heading, Stephen Jones, Mindy LePere, Ricardo Martin, Lenelle Parker, Dana Payne, Michael Phillips, and Joanne Sanneh.

Classroom Connect, an Internet site, linked me with forty-eight hundred classrooms. By advertising in *Poets and Writers Magazine* and with the Society of Children's Book Writers and Illustrators, I gained access to other individuals who would be interested in the project nationwide. Among the many people who helped me with submissions from across the country were Sheerly Avni of *YO!,* Nancy Barnby, Robert Boone of Young Chicago Authors, Paul Dunlap, Janet

Elliot, Gloria Evangelista, Jean Frankenfeld, Alfred Gomez, Meg Spencer Gorman, Traci Gourdine of the California State Summer School for the Arts, Steven Hulme, Joseph McCarren of Slippery Rock University, Judith Michaels, author of *Risking Intensity: Reading and Writing Poetry with High School Students,* Ann Munro, Christina Pacosz, Coach Parks, Alma G. Perez, Marsha Pittelkow, and Maura Vaughn. In the final stretch, Robin Reagler of WITS (Writers In The Schools) and her staff went out of their way to help me gather permissions from WITS authors in Houston.

Special thanks to my consultant Maria Damon, a writer and a professor of literature at the University of Minnesota, who was dedicated to the book and spent countless hours working on it with me. Thank you as well to my consultant Lorraine Bates Noyes, a writer, who generously solicited and evaluated submissions. Both Maria and Lorraine offered encouragement when I most needed it.

My sons — James, Thomas, and David — helped me keep my adult viewpoint out of each stage of the process and gave me advice about selections. My husband, Douglas Franco, offered valuable suggestions, and Marjorie Franco assisted with the editing of the stories.

Most important of all were my consultants in their teens and early twenties. Sam Doniach, Quantedius Hall, Stephan Johnson, Benjamin Martin, Sean McDonnell, Mike McGaraghan, Sean Mitchell, David Persyko, Daniel Raburn, and Shysuaune Taylor read and responded to each piece in the first draft. Their insightful feedback was integral to the selection process.

Working with my editor, Mary Lee Donovan, was a wonderful experience. She understood the book, was willing to take chances, and had a genuine respect and sensitivity for the authors. Associate editor Kara LaReau was insightful and supportive. Amy Rennert, my agent, understood my vision and believed in the project from the start.

Thank you especially to all the writers who trusted me enough to submit their poems, stories, and essays. Whether or not your work made it into the final collection, you played an important part in making this book possible.

YOU HEAR ME?

once
I was the son of Mother with a capital M.
once I knew what I was made of.
once I had a crown of stars
once I had a golden heart
once I was a bird and a rock and a splash and a gurgle
and I laughed like a lily
I was a naked little flower
growing out of my mother's belly.

I used to own a tomato red hat
with tomato red sweats
and a tomato red turtle-neck.
I used to stand on the deck
when my grandma still smoked cigarettes.
I used to watch moths in the garden
visiting the evening primrose
on full moon nights.

I was a little frog in my underwear
chasing snakes in a muddy pond
I was a little soft-faced boy
making bird's nests out of rice grass
I was full of clouds and sun
once
I was a brand new star.

Nick Ross-Rhudy, age 17

TOPIC 1: INTRODUCTIONS

Hi My Name is Tom
(Sounds good:
    Direct
    Honest
    Telling
    Humble)

My favorite Color is Blue
    (Yikes!
      No —
    Take back
    Lie
    Nerves
    Panic
    Upset
    Fluster)

I Like Blue
    (Okay!
    Good comeback)

How Are You?

Thomas Andrade, age 18

FRONT SEAT RIDER

Riding in a car,
I like to be the one to drive,
unlike my brother who always sits
in the back seat. He enjoys
just riding along, free to take in
scenes along the way, girls
and all that, rather than having
to watch where he's going.
He doesn't like
to ride with me, though.
He accuses me of doing
seventy-five to a hundred mph right in
the neighborhood. I admit I
drive fast, but not that fast, although
I like to get a whiff of burnt rubber
every now and then. I'd be
grounded for a year if my mother
caught me driving as fast as that.
I'm a front seat rider all the way.
If I ride at all, it's got to be
behind the wheel.

Triston L. Dunnett, age 15

Just because I love darkness
Doesn't mean I'm depressed
Doesn't mean I can't love
Doesn't mean I'm blind.
Just because I love my Mom
Doesn't mean I'm not a rebel
Doesn't mean I can't love others
Doesn't mean I'm a mama's boy.
Just because I act psycho
Doesn't mean I need medication
Doesn't mean I can't be compassionate
Doesn't mean I don't cry.

Marcel Mendoza, age 16

JOKER

You would be surprised
To know that the funny man
Is also the sad man
Like a clown fallen from his stilts.

     But this is his career
     Never will a joker feel secure in a serious environment
     He will keep telling jokes
     Never will a joker be secure in his insecurities
     He will keep telling jokes.

In the process of getting out of a hole
A hole I dug for myself
A bottomless pit
I will die . . .
Like the product of a pun
A misunderstanding.
The saddest joke . . .

     A clown lying by his stilts, full of regret.

Michael Tobias Bloom, age 16

DARK CELLAR

I like to hide in my dark damp cellar
Where rats scurry across the cold cement floor.
I don't know why I like to hide in my dark damp cellar.
All I know is that anger and sorrow
Evaporate into clouds of air
And bad thoughts disintegrate
When I'm there.

Every boy should have a cellar.

Joshua White, age 12

HE SHAVED HIS HEAD

He shaved his head to release his imagination.
He did it to get a tattoo on his shiny head.
He did it to lose his normality.
He did it to become a freak.
He did it because he was angry.
He did it to make people angry.
He did it for himself.

Rene Ruiz, age 13

BROKEN GLASS

crazy mad
mad like a vulture
no prey

i am a soldier
wounded in duty

i'm angry, man
you hear me?
angry
like a second place loser

loser, man

can you dig it?
can you feel me, winner?

i am not weird
i don't hold grudges
or sing in the shower
or chew rusty razors

do you?

i break glass
i cut it, man
i am able to cut glassy stares with sharper ones

believe me i'll do it
i'll handle it

i'm crazy mad

you can't stop the rain
or the reign

Joshua Bonds, age 17

INSTRUCTIONS FOR LIFE

Catch the football and make sure you score a touchdown; jump into the mud and make certain it is enjoyable; rip your jeans and tear your shirts; bleed on the field of glory and take it like a man; grind the grass stains into your clothes; order a hot dog at a baseball game; watch the Super Bowl and tell everyone about the play in the second half to prove you watched it; root for the home team; get hurt but don't cry; hide your emotions; pick yourself up when you are down; watch violent movies and crave blood and destruction. This is how to act tough on the outside; this is how you act in front of the guys. Slick your hair back with your father's gel just the right way to catch the eye of the girl next to you; don't burp; act like a gentleman; wear clothes that make you look cool; walk a walk that shows the girls how suave you are; act mature; protect your sister if she needs help. This is how you act in front of the girls. Do well in school; get straight A's because you have to get into a good college. This is how to succeed; this is how to be prosperous; this is how to be happy and live life to the fullest.

Brando, age 15

THE TORCH

Where was I when they were passing the torch
when they were all
getting some action out in the bush
getting some action behind a very green graffiti garage
getting some action out in the goddamned field
When they were all
getting their jock straps monogrammed gold
When they were all sipping sweaty, hard brews
Where was I when our fathers were teaching us
how to cover our cocks with barbed wire
teaching us how to make love
and orgasmic war
Where was I when we were boys becoming
greasy, bald-headed deacons and
finger-fucking commandos Praise the Lord
when we were boys becoming
fat-breasted, gold-buttoned, white-wig financiers
and the people who control the mail God bless America
Where was I when they were
boys sodomizing pilgrims and indians
and all the horses in between and leaving them for dead
Where was I when we were
playing spin-the-bottle at the never-ending parties
with girls in semen-colored dresses
pulled all the way over their heads and
who seemed to cum all night

Where was I when they were pissing inside
of their pretty alcoholic wives
When they were dancing naked homosexual rain dances
in the locker rooms all across the American galaxy and
smearing pricked fingers together swearing allegiance
to the covering of each other's ass
When they were taking shit breaks from the divine Law
as only real men can
When they turned Christ into toilet bowl cleaner
and Buddha into a synonym for the pussy hole and
Allah into abracadabra and
eventually a puff of cigarette smoke.
shit.
Where was I when we were growing invisible public hair,
taking the last drop of milk from the cow
graduating from Superman lunch boxes to
plumber's ass cracks and tool boxes
Where was I when all my brothers passed the torch before
me?
Where was I
and why can't I stop screaming?

Michael R. Jackson, age 17

MY POCKETS AIN'T THAT PHAT

I
   rotate to the rhythm
   of a ghetto
         grape
         jimbe
         voice
my step
is faaaaarrr to the left
and I
      don't
wanna keep up
      with Generation
            X-pense
            X-plore
            X-cite
            X-press myself
my groove
            clues of
reds, blacks, and blues

I
   don't
      wear nothing
of a

Nautica
Eddie Bauer
　Nike
　Fila
　Timbo-
　land
　Rockport
　Mike Jordan
　　　scent
　My clothes
　　　stay big
　　　Kmart cool
　　　Target fresh

I'm
　not a
hip hop
Dred
retro
　4-pierced brotha

Don't wanna be wrapped
up in '70s leather
polyester Afro
　　zones

My hair is
          not
     tightly faded
     brown-skinned
     flawless, suave
My ride ain't
     a drop top
     bassed
     hydraulic
     screamin'
     pimp wagon
My tongue
          was not meant to
M.A.C.

My thoughts are
tightly wound
          about
makin'
     one
          Mrs.
               mine.

I'm cream
          neutral
          chills

of gray
        brown patterns
Forgive me for not
speaking.
            My dance of rejection
            freaks me
            breathless.

In a room of
        human collages
I'd rather sit
        and converse
with anger, happiness,
        my personality's
                offspring

I'm not
down with impressing
        anyone's impression
of an urban hip hop image
No, that stereotype
        doesn't move me
My words
        complement those
            that welcome
them.

'Til then
    they stay
colorfully quiet with
        a lot of a
        little
        to
        say!

Shysuaune T. Taylor, age 18

M.A.C. — flirt with every woman that comes my way

ODE TO MY HAIR TAIL

My hair tail is like a snake
wrapped around my neck.

It feels like a spider
crawling on my neck.

In the dark you cannot see
my hair tail because it's black.
In the sun it looks brown.

It decorates the back of my head.

When my sister tries to braid
it, she gets mad because it's long,
and it looks skinny from the
bottom, and she thinks she'll never
finish.

Some people think
that I am in a gang and
throw me gang signs.

In the mirror my hair tail looks
shiny, and I can see how
long it is.

I think I'll cut my hair tail
when it's a little bigger. I'll
save it and take it to
San Juan, Texas, and
leave it in a church.

Rigo Landin, 17

It all started in second grade. There was this kid and he would jump on my desk and chair. He also would call me inappropriate things. My teacher would say, Stay away from him. I said, *He* comes to *me.* She didn't care.

In third grade people were calling me a girl so I went down a hill and pulled down my pants to prove I wasn't. I was suspended for three days. After that it got a lot worse. Kids hit me and swore at me. One day at recess, some kids were chasing me and I went down a hill and about thirty kids beat me up big time.

In fourth grade, people were cooling down on me a little. But still, every time I went to the office to report on some kids, they wouldn't do anything. So I started saying things back to the kids. They went to the office and reported on me. I got in trouble. One time, the assistant principal carried me all the way to the office. My mom would check on me every day. At the end of the year things were starting to look up for me. I was going to go to a different school in fifth grade. The principal said that she would talk to the other kids that were going to the new school. During the summer I was diagnosed with Tourette syndrome.

In fifth grade I was in my new school. But the kids from my old school who were there spread everything that had happened. So most of the kids in the school were mean to me. I reported on them every day, but nobody did anything. When kids reported on me, I got in big trouble. Most of the time they would lie to the people in the office. I had maybe one friend in that school.

In sixth grade, it was bad again. I was beat up by some mean kid. People were calling me every bad word there is. They did a talk in my class to explain that I have Tourette and what it does to me. It helped a little at first, but it didn't last. In the bathrooms, there were no locks on the stall doors, so kids kicked in the door every time I went in there. I had to go to the bathroom in the nurse's office.

In seventh grade I was suspended two times the first week of school so I had to be in the quiet room at all times. People asked me why I was always in there. I told them, Because of you. It lasted until Christmas vacation. After Christmas vacation, I went to a special school program. It was good for the rest of the year.

1999–2000 I'm in eighth grade now in the program and it's great. I hope my story will show how hard it is to have Tourette syndrome.

Nick Sletten, age 13

Tourette syndrome is a neurobiological disorder. Symptoms include impulsive behavior, embarrassing tics, anxiety, and phobias. Verbal tics can include swearing and other socially unacceptable language. Understanding on the part of others, medical treatment, and learning coping strategies can lessen the anxiety for the individual with Tourette syndrome.

I AM

I am the hated one,
Spreader of the disease,
Carrying the blame unjustly.
I am the dying innocent.
I am the ungodly thing
Preached against in church—
Preached against in politics.
I am the loathed,
I am the shunned,
I am feared,
I am gay.

I am dying innocent,
I am Goddess,
I am God.
I am an unborn child.
I am a dying mother.
I am the blood from your wound.
I am living with you,
I am dying because of you.

James Balzer, age 14

CARABAO DREAMS

how how the carabao said to me in a dream
   refute the conspiring evils
   prove the strength that wills your breath
   hold tightly to poetry and loved ones
   as a book would bind its pages
   share your story through art and song
   fix your eyes on the stars so your voice
    can be heard
     "taas noo, iho, taas noo!"

you *are* more than
   what they say
   what they think
   what they see

pinoy **is** more than
   brown and alibata
   barongs and tinikling
   pansit and Goldilocks
    you will understand

queer **is** more than
   cocks and A.I.D.S.
   white men and the Castro
   June and pride marches
    you will understand

life **is** more than
> angst and depression
> money and aspiration
> wanting and loneliness
>> ***you will understand***

how how the carabao said to me
> tell the people your story
> don't think an amendment frees your
> speech
> if they cover their ears and refuse to listen
> yell if you have to
> you do not have a choice
> this is not a request
> you need to be heard

how how the carabao said to me
> rush out into the world in perfect
> surrender
> give in to the sun as she licks your face
> and thighs
> offer no words when the winds
> whip at your backside
> respect the moon
> yield up limber arms in reverence to
> the stars
> for darkness is also a gift
> and silence can be a friend

go out into the world and do these things
and you will understand

how how the carabao said to me
sadness is not the absence of happiness
but your incapacity to witness its presence
your soul is not just a bird taking up
wings
your soul is the sea
your spirit is the shore
your mind is the black expanse
that births planets and consumes galaxies
you are not only part of the revolution
but you are the revolution
when you stop building comfortable walls
and notice that your feet are planted
on the same ground on which millions
have stood
you will understand
you will understand
you will understand

you *are* more than pansit
A.I.D.S.
and depression

how how the carabao said to me in a dream
this is just a dream

these are just my words
breathe life into them
assign them feet
make them real
how how the carabao said to me

how

how

Timothy Arevalo, age 18

carabao — water buffalo
"taas noo, iho, taas noo!" — "Look up, son, look up!"
pinoy — a Filipino person
alibata — ancient Tagalog script
barong — traditional Filipino shirt
tinikling — traditional Filipino dance
pansit — rice noodles

JUST LIKE ME

Black describes me.
My moods, my personality.
Black is a color that everyone likes.
Black is subtle,
Not too flashy, not too boring.
Black is power, authority.
Black moves like air.
Close your eyes, it's everywhere.
Black is nonchalant.
Black's carefree.
Nothing phases this color.
Black's hard as steel.

Black is my best friend.
Because we're just alike,
Plain, basic, understated,
Unlike a red or orange or yellow.
We don't brighten up a room.
We bring a coolness
That can't be produced by another.

Stone-faced is our expression.

Relaxed is our mood,

Our state of mind.

We stand alone,

But we can mix

With all people, all colors.

Lawan Mitchell, age 16

OUT OF MY LIFE

I want my grandmother
to stop sending me to the store
with fifty dollars worth of bottles
not sold in Michigan.

I want my grandfather
to stop telling the same war stories
that begin at breakfast
and end after dinner.

I want the Kool-Aid
to stop disappearing in one hour.
I want the ice trays
to stay filled.

I want the only bathroom
in the house
to be free for me
when nature calls.

I want big Ms. Whitaker
to stop wearing that frizzy wig
and pink dress that barely covers
what only her husband needs to see.

I want this to be
the last stanza of this poem
so I can burn this worn down pencil
and inhale the ashes.

Corey Edge, age 17

SLEEP

I woke up pissed this morning.
No motivation to get out of bed.
So many negative thoughts in my head.
I try to shake it off like everything is okay,
but the empty feeling in my gut won't go away.
My mind is at rest while I lie in bed,
which is better than lying to my soul outside today.
I roll over and retreat back to the safety of my dreams,
which will sedate the memory of
unfinished homework and a test at lunch.
Now I don't have to deal with the pain of fake smiles,
empty eyes, and pointless conversation.
Society seems to think I can't sleep my way through life,
albeit I had no regrets today.

Kyle Blanchard, age 16

Fuck this shit, up the ass, I don't think I'll ever pass. It's fucking crap. I don't believe. I think that I'll just fucking leave. The teachers suck, the food just blows, society has reached new lows. We sit and stare all fucking day. And though it's public, we still pay.

I hate this fucking bullshit. I don't want to take it.

It's fucking bunk. We're not prepared. The grown-up world makes me scared. Inspirational posters on the wall— why won't that kitty fucking fall? A fight-free campus is required, but child molesters are not fired. They want the school clean and drug free, but I know a teacher who does speed.

I hate this fucking bullshit. I don't want to take it.

The PE teachers are insane, their methods can't be called humane. Smoking bud across the street, but hey— our football can't be beat! The jocks, they run the fucking school, chew dip all day, act real cool. Everybody annoys me. Someone is gonna get beat.

Kenny Weiss, age 17

I NEVER TOLD THIS TO ANYONE

There is a secret that I have told to no one.
The burning house that stood blazing on the hill,
the house that was occupied by a kind old man,
burned to the ground in front of my eyes.
No words were *ever* spoken
and only I know the truth.
I never told even this much to anyone.

Maurice Beaman, age 16

I'LL BE HERE

Go find yourself a listening ear,
And let it know all that you fear.

If the ear you seek cannot be found,
Don't shove your feelings to the ground.

Don't give up and run away;
Try again another day.

If nothing works and no one's there,
I know someone who will care.

I'll always be here for you,
Should you need someone to talk to.

Come and talk, come and cry,
Don't stop until your eyes are dry.

Once it's out, you've nothing to fear,
As long as you know, I'll always be here.

David Ho, age 16

FACES

Faces pass by at 35 mph
staring at you, laughing at you
wanting you, intrigued by you
loving you, hating you
giving you a smile that says, "Good morning"
giving you a look that says, "Stop looking at me."

You look for someone you know
your brother, your grandma, your ex-girlfriend
the president, your barber, Neil Armstrong,
Jon Voight, Michael Jordan, or Leslie Nielsen
the guy you saw in a Subway eating a tuna foot-long
the girl who sold you peanuts at Wrigley Field
the lover you wish for after a hard day
the asshole who stole your bicycle when you were nine.

But you're lost, a stranger among strangers
no idea who you are or why you're here
just that you're alone, lost in this city of faces.

Dan Gallagher, age 16

In this darkness, I stand still,
Alone and cold.
The night drags on.
The sleep of over one hundred years.
No one seems to care,
But the darkness it will bear
The loves of time gone by.

People stare and ask
What my weariness means,
But they will never know,
No one will ever know,
Because all they do is stare
And see that I am going nowhere,
But never try to come along.

Jared Ryan Jackson Lowry, age 17

You've asked about me. I am a 20-year-old native Houstonian. I was a happy child from divorced parents. My parents divorced when I was two, but they always got along very well. One of the strangest things about my mother and father is that they were second cousins. I'm not *challenged* or anything. In fact, the probability that there will be a deformity from the coupling of second cousins is the same as people not related at all, 1 in 23.

My mother is a great person. An ex-hippie born and raised here in Texas, she has seen and done many things. She hitchhiked to California in 1969 at age 18. She saw the Doors, Led Zeppelin, and the original Black Sabbath in concert, not together of course. She has raised me well and has influenced me in many ways.

My father was a great guy. He was raised in El Paso, Texas, along with his identical twin brother and three other brothers and sisters. Like my mother, he had some hippie tendencies. His first vehicle was a Volkswagen microbus that he and his twin brother bought for $450. My father was pretty cool and quiet. A little over two years ago, a massive coronary killed him at the age of forty-three.

I was grief-stricken. Since the divorce, I had never seen my dad on a daily basis, but it was hard to deal with his really being gone. Shortly after his death, I was awarded $62,000 in life insurance. That money was my downfall.

Always a fairly poor person financially, I was overwhelmed by the money. Instead of saving it, or investing it, I spent it—in one and a half years. I bought a 1981 Jeep and a 1972 Volkswagen bus. I got Heavy into drugs. Cocaine, pills of all kinds went into my system, but the worst was heroin. That monster cost me all of my money and the trust of many of my friends. Since then, I've been to rehab, I'm going to college, and I have a good job. Hopefully, I'm now on the right track.

Jared Ryan Jackson Lowry, age 20

Jared wrote this essay in the spring of 1996. In the fall of 1997, the "monster" took him.

CHANT

smoke
choke
riverside dope
greens
funk
pump in the trunk
girls, boys
beer & liquor
cigarettes
hotels
weeds & strippers
fat girls
little girls
girls with whiskers
fine girls
pretty girls
girls with cute sisters
pimps, ballers
players & G's
just another day
in the D

Tommie Spivey, age 18

BLACK BOY BLUES

baby black boy learns his a,b,c's
baby black boy learns his a,b,c's
A,B,C,R,A,C,K Recipes
Boiling water, baking soda
Burning broken wire hangers.

mama don't know granny is into plague retail
mama don't know granny is into plague retail
Watch baby black hands trace
deadly outlines of overdosed
souls quivering on the floor

Baby black boy eyes watch
dream smoke rise
from glass
pipes
Baby black boy eyes watch
dream smoke rise
from glass
pipes
Burning away bills, food, hungry baby mouths

baby boy black learns his 1,2,3's
baby boy black learns his 1,2,3's
1,2,3 ounces of Cocaine
to be made into

rock
    crystallized
      worlds
to be made into
   rock
     crystallized
      worlds

sing the song of make believe baby boy black
sing the song of make believe baby boy black
as you watch the gun
being put to granny's head
and she
clicks
and she
clicks
and she
clicks

  make believe
you are unaware
make believe
you are not scared
make believe
you don't know the recipe
for
     horror

Shysuaune T. Taylor, age 19

The trombones slap me in the face with their high-life beats, and the piano's glamorous tunes tap me on my shoulder and whisper in my ear. As I look down into the Juke-Joint from my bedroom floor, rotted house, rotted life, plain rotten seems forgotten as the music plays and the beats go down to the rhythm of my heart's pound. There's a Harlem Renaissance in my head, there's a Harlem Renaissance in my head.

Through the floor a light, where the music roared, overtakes the darkness that surrounds me as I look through this floorboard. I can see the hoppin' and a dancin' and the suave men a prancin' around the young ladies who stand stunning on the floor . . .

The music stops, the poet stands up, and with each turn of the page, his mind's thoughts he will emancipate and everybody in the room he will captivate. His pen his only weapon with which injustice he must eradicate. As I look down into the Juke-Joint from my bedroom floor, rotted house, rotted life, plain rotten seems forgotten as the music plays and the beats go down to the rhythm of my thoughts' pound. There's a Harlem Renaissance in my head.

Let your ink run rampant, Langston Hughes. Let your fingers tickle the ivories forever, Duke. At every moment history being made in my own personal Juke-Joint. I lean my ears to hear even closer and find my mind in a past tense, opening my eyes to see beauty, but surrounded by pure silence. There's a Harlem Renaissance in my head, a Harlem Renaissance in my head.

Maurice E. Duhon, Jr., age 17

WHAT I AM
(IN THE EYES OF MY FATHER)

I am nothing
in the eyes
of my father.

When I get
good grades
he doesn't say

anything, not
one good word.
When I didn't

get into a top
high school
he said I was

nothing, never
going to be
nothing. I am

beaten down
from heaven
by the shaft

of my father.
It feels like
a bullwhip

going across
my back
every time

he puts me,
beats me
down, down.

Dwight Beavers, age 17

ODE TO CARING

Careless child I am
wandering off into the night
I make my mother stir at small hours
she makes herself
words in books fused together
like so many lies to soothe her angst
lies of where I've been
when I'll return
my father wishes my integrity
he doesn't know I wish the same
who knows in what completeness I'll return
but the propaganda is posted
and the party rages
someday the dissension will end
until then she'll read the lies

Benjamin D. Martin, age 17

———————

Sometimes
But not always
Well hardly ever it seems
Something is truly fulfilling.
A shame.

Michael Tobias Bloom, age 16

DOES MY MOTHER LOOK LIKE THIS?

Is she light-skinned
or is she brown?

Does she smile
or does she frown?

Is my mother tall
or is she short?

Is she a quitter
or a good sport?

Does my mother look like
a person who would

leave four sons and a daughter
and go to another place?

What does she look like?
Can you picture her face?

Seth Chappell, age 14

WORDS ON HANDS

(FOR LESLIE REESE)

Her voice danced black rhythms
Sunday dresses, old school tunes;
Funky Nassau, Temptations
That doo-wop group
That always hung
Out on the corner of
51st Street. Singin'
till the liquor store closed
45 records, 8-track tapes skippin'
skippin' until you
put that piece of paper
between the 8-track
and the stereo in a just-right position.

Her actions were painters splashing
Little black girls in pastels
Blue, yellow, pink Easter
Dresses, with white stockings
forbidden to run.
She taught me how to
write the smell of Grandma's greens,
chittlins, turkey whose reign
was always religious brown.

She wrote auntie's apple pie
like the sun going down, down
down till moonlight
shone on Uncle Junebug's bottle
of Cognac.

She made my brain sweat.
　　　Work out your
words with actions she said.
Make the tears of a
broken child smear
your ink, make the
joy of a grandmother
be the fragrance
of your voice. Hear Mama
smacking her child
with words that taste
like morning pancakes.
My performing teacher

pulled a me
　　　out of me
who was a dancer
an artist, whose actions
spoke words.

Shysuaune T. Taylor, age 17

I was a little curious about why my divorced parents had taken me to lunch on a hot, August day, but halfway through the lunch I found out. My father wanted to tell me he was gay, and that his friend Dave was actually his lover.

I was shocked. All I could do was concentrate on eating. Although I acted polite and understanding at the restaurant, my thoughts were really somewhere else, and it wasn't until my mother and I were alone that night that I began to unload my feelings.

"How could he do this to me?" I asked over and over. Though my mother and my father divorced when I was just seven, this new reality felt like too big a burden. How could I go anywhere with my father and Dave? What if someone I knew saw us? I could just imagine how cruel they might be, "Hey, did you know Jaime's dad's a fag?"

Not only was I afraid somebody might see us, I was afraid that my dad and Dave might display affection toward each other in front of me. To a sixteen-year-old boy, this would be disgusting.

As time went on, I decided that the best thing to do was to remain silent. I would not tell a soul, no matter what. After almost a year, however, I had to get this secret off my chest. I told my best friend, and to my surprise he didn't have a problem with my secret at all.

His reaction changed me. Was it such a big deal? Did the fact that my dad was homosexual actually matter? The more I thought about it, the more I understood, and the happier I became for my dad. He had found someone he cared about and loved.

Through the two years it's taken me to reach this point, I have discovered a lot about personal relationships. At first, I was always worried about what people would think of me. I have come to realize that I don't care what ignorant people think. Why would I want to be friends with anyone who would judge me based on prejudice toward my father?

Telling me about his relationship must have been one of the hardest things my dad has done. He placed himself at a crossroads of rejection or acceptance; a risk he took that shows me how much he truly loves me.

Jaime Daryl Marconette, age 18

I REFUSE

When I see the word *father*, the first person that comes to mind is myself. I am the father of a six-month-old girl who can light up the room when she smiles. Don't all parents feel this way about their children, or is it just me? All fathers don't stay around their kids, though. It seems to take bravery or some miracle for them to stick it out and see to their kids' well being. To be a father is more than a responsibility; it is a job. Tradition says that a father is the provider, not an easy role to play when you're still in high school, working low income jobs. Still, I do it for the good of my daughter, my creation, my seed. I refuse to be a deadbeat dad because no excuse is a good enough excuse to abandon your own creation.

Steven Hill, age 18

———————

What happened Papa
What happened
Was it something I said
did
became?

Joshua Bonds, age 17

ASCENSION

My creation
was the solidification
of cries into pride
the first generation unadorned
by thorns
but when I was born
I was torn from my mother's chest

and they took me, melted my spirit
and squeezed until i was drained
morphing my frame
into a hollow lyric

I tightrope walk on rugged course
trying to fill myself back up
an empty volcano ready to erupt
holding hollow heart as cup
in hands
panhandling
for my spirit

but it cost too much to be a clone
so i took my hollow heart trying to pay
for what i thought was home
but they caught me sellin' nickel bags
of funk

in culture free zones
where the kids are drones
and have bones
made of dollar bills

and i spoke on these ills
and the police beat me until
i was unconscious enough to be read
my rights

then 6 knights
began to shine a light in my face
causing my subconscious to grate
dichotomous thoughts

separating cross from crucifixion
understanding the refractions of
mother's prism
putting false benedictions
under inquisition
and making the ultimate decision
to heal subconscious incision
made by colonizers
when they conspired
to take identity and land from fore
fathers
and morph it into tabula rasa

and they tried to make me cop a plea
and live my life in dependence
but fuck the 5th amendment
because I am the 7th descendant
of Truth

and my thoughts were dead until hope
made my words living proof
so the knights prepared the noose
and the scalpel for my castration
but their definition of manhood was so
complacent
they had not a clue to the gift i had
given

or the one i received
and they couldn't see
that this tree
was hanging on to me
and i was finally one with my brethren

so now i sit in the womb of heaven
telling GOD my story
and she rubs my head gently
and says you are loved
and can never be empty

Biko Eisen-Martin, age 16

———

I don't
Know what it is
I'll know when it comes
But I'll never be waiting here
For death.

Chorus Bishop, age 15

THE BUS STOP

When I woke up this morning I walked to my bus stop. A boy and a girl I kind of knew were arguing on the people's porch I set on every morning. The girl was raising hell about going to the doctor. I guess she was mad because no one took her to the doctor. She had a little baby in her arms. She left her house and walked down the street with the baby. Then the boy walked after her. I guess he stole the baby out of her arms. He walked back up the street holding the baby.

The next thing I saw, the girl came back to her house and took her baby from the boy. The boy said, "I got something for you!" He punched the girl and she fell with the baby in her arms. A couple of times. I was standing on the stair. "Hold my baby!" she said to me. I grabbed the baby and she punched the boy back in his face. Then the girl's brother came down the stairs and grabbed them apart. I gave the baby back to the girl. Then it started up again. It was a mess! The boy dropped his beeper. I picked it up and gave it to him. He said, "Thanks!"

My bus came.

Fred Brown, age 14

PEOPLE GOT MORE

Where me and Earnest went today,
seems like people got more
than what we have.
Black people down here won't
go to school or get jobs.
Those people get more money
put in their community.
They want us to stay back and live in the ghetto.
But it's not up to me.
It's up to *us* to stay in school
and get jobs
and make K.C. worth something.

Fred Brown, age 14

K.C. — Kansas City

I WANT

To know
If there's a ghetto
In heaven.

Troy Williams, age 16

ENVY

May I ask you something?
Why are you following me?
Every time I turn around
You are there telling me
something to wish for:

       his blue Mercedes
       his caramel girlfriend
       his Bloomfield house
       his paycheck.

Leave me alone.

Kyle L. White, age 17

MY LIFE

I live my life
Like quiet mice
Sometimes I think I'm way too nice.

I have no friends
But that's gonna end
I wish my uncle wasn't in the pen.

I have two sisters
One I don't like
Sometimes she makes me want to smack her all night.

I have a car
It's nice and blue
I like driving it 'cause it's fun to do.

One day I will drive it
From home to school
Oh I have a car that's nice and blue.

I love my mother
Like a son should
I'll always be there for her any way I could.

I have a job
For that I thank my aunt and God
I work very hard to keep my little job.

This is my life
I hope you think it's nice
If you don't I'll still be all right.

DeQon L Abner, age 16

BUMMING THROUGH PITTSBURGH? MAYBE NOT.

Hey, where are you going?
Where will you be in five to ten years?
Is it college, career, or do you really care
with your dark baggy clothing
and whacked out hair,
your face, an unfinished puzzle.
The moon only shines for those who request it.

Because the moon only shines for those who request it,
your face is an unfinished puzzle
with your whacked out hair
and dark baggy clothing.
Do you really care? Is it college, career —
where will you be in five to ten years?
Hey, where are you going?

Antony E. W. Kirkland, age 18

NEIGHBORHOOD WATCH

My neighborhood's filled with people who burn tires to
show off in front of other people with sweet cars. Stray
dogs run the street, pit bulls and rottweilers barking in
backyards. People stand on the street corner for no apparent
reason. Kids play football with pop bottles. My neighbor
Mr. Huffman comes home every day at six with his dog
at the fence waiting for him. My pit bull Damien in the
basement barks, thinking someone's in the backyard or in
the house who's not supposed to be. My brother Andre tells
him to shut up 'cause he's trying to go to sleep. My uncle
Clarence is in the back finishing the dog house. Pit bulls
come in every color in the backyards on my block. People
I've never seen before gamble on the porch. My mother
fusses at Damien for not shutting up. People race up and
down the street for entertainment. Weed smokers and dope
dealers. At night, gunshots, police sirens, fire sirens echo
from blocks away. Ms. Carter, an elderly woman, is outside
almost every day watering the grass. Watch out: she'll fuss
at you if you step on her grass.

Troy Williams, age 16

THE BEST CHRISTMAS OF ONASIS RODRIGUEZ

My best Christmas was two years ago because someone my dad knew at work invited us to his apartment to celebrate. When my dad and I got to the apartment, we marveled that it was so pretty. All the decorations were nice because the guy my dad knew from work had put a lot of effort into them. There were candles, presents, lights, and lots of food. My dad and I sat on the sofa. We met some people at the party we didn't know, friends and relatives of our host. We all ate chicken sandwiches and drank sodas. I couldn't help staring at the tree. It was decorated with lights, ornaments, a star on top, and especially, presents underneath.

When it was time to open the presents, my dad and I didn't have any to open because nobody really knew us. You might think that I was sad. But here's the best part of all: a lady at the party went to her room and came back with a present and gave it to me. I didn't know her but she was nice to me.

But I prefer a Gameboy or Playstation for a gift rather than a shirt. My dad didn't care about himself. He was happy that I got a present. My dad felt as good as I did.

At twelve o'clock, it was time for my dad and me to go home and go to sleep. On Sunday, I wore the shirt.

Onasis Hafid Rodriguez, age 15

As I sat, awaiting my match with the man known as Tripod, I had my "wrestling epiphany." My match with Tripod exemplified what I felt was the central dilemma in wrestling and made me realize that wrestling was not the sport for me.

The match with Tripod was no ordinary match — it was greatly complicated by the absence of his left leg. This complication made the bout one of the most intensely confusing experiences of my life. If I won the match, I would have faced the ignominy of having beaten up a disabled person. If I lost the match, I would have suffered the humiliation of having been out-wrestled by a guy with one leg. Surely, there could not be much dignity in either outcome.

The match was highly unorthodox. Tripod had an unusual repertoire of moves that effectively compensated for his disability. While Tripod used his specially designed pinning combinations on me, I succeeded in doing little but look shocked and confused. Tripod's competence as a wrestler was my only consolation as I returned, easily beaten, to my heckling teammates.

My match with Tripod taught me that I was not nor would ever be a wrestler and resulted in a temporary general distaste for athletic competition. Although wrestling a one-legged guy is not a common experience, the same dilemma presents itself in every competition. In victory you humiliate another, and in defeat another humiliates you. Realizing that wrestling can be a losing proposition in both victory and defeat changed my life significantly.

The world of sports organizes competition into wins and losses. Through my match with Tripod, I realized that winning and losing are only two of many possibilities and that each competition has the potential for an infinite number of outcomes. In my match with Tripod, the public outcome was less important than the outcome of my internal struggle. I now coach a Hillview Middle School girls' basketball team. Our primary goals, taught to me by the players, are pride, respect, and good sportsmanship.

Michael Kinsey, age 17

FIRST LOVE

Trained to return to my hand
like a yo-yo with no strings,
you burn nets to cinders,
kiss the backboard.

At night on the floor
next to me,
you press against desire,
waiting for the even rotation
of my touch.

I hear your voice calling me.
I am only twelve but
I can still grasp
the motion, the smoothness
of your bare skin,

how you love the way
my fingertips slide
softly across your body.
I am hypnotized every time
we touch.

This is not love, but addiction.
You blaze past my opponents,
but I am on fire.

Stephan Johnson, age 17

FOUL

Hearing cries of "Foul! Foul!" on the basketball court
Playing hard, sweating
Feeling dizzy and high, as if on crack
Leaving the court, funk in my nose
My funky, ball-playin', leaving-pop-at-the-hoop butt
Being chased by dogs out of oblivion
Mom telling me not to sit on the furniture
'Cause I'm even more funky now

Hussian Fry, age 16

I LOVE TO HEAR

how women say
my name —

"Tito . . ."
"Tito . . ."

— saying it
over and over

as if they don't want
to let go.

Tito D. Tate, age 15

THE GIRL I LIKE

I saw this girl on my way
home. She is everything
I want in a girl. A girl who
makes me smile when she smiles,
a girl who speaks what she feels.
She makes my heart skip like
a street beat, happy.

Ronnie Ross, age 16

AMOR DE DOS CULTURAS

Cuando en dos culturas
hay amor, que es diferente,
en las dos culturas encuentras paz y amistad
y cuando te enamoras
no importa de que sangre es, si no la sangre
que hay dentro de tu corazón.

LOVE BETWEEN TWO CULTURES

Between two cultures you find
a love that is different,
Between two cultures you find peace and friendship,
and when you fall in love
it doesn't matter of what blood, just the blood
that is in your heart.

Juan C. Medina Arias, age 18

Sunlight bouncing from hair
light walk, bright countenance
jealousy is mine

DTB, age 17

I watch you
Undress me with your eyes
Take off my shirt
Kiss my chest
You'll use me
so.
I can't stop you
Unzipping my pants
You don't know
I cringe every time you touch me.

Bryan Phillips, age 16

SATISFACTION OF AN ORANGE

Two boys sat on the edge of the lawn next to their classroom. The sun was high, making small shadows on the grass around them. Other students lounged not far off, in small groups of three or four. One of the boys took an orange from his backpack, tearing into its skin with his uncut fingernail.

"The most satisfying thing in life is an orange," he stated, gently pulling the skin away, splitting the fruit in half.

"No it's not," argued the other.

The first boy pushed a whole slice between his lips. "It's soft and juicy and sweet in your mouth," he said.

"It's not the most satisfying thing," repeated the other, watching his friend caress a slice with his tongue.

"What is then?" the friend asked, chewing, turning to look at the other boy.

"Pussy," he stated, glancing at his pack, then back up at his friend.

"How would you know?" exclaimed the first, tearing another slice, popping it into his mouth.

"I dunno," shrugged the second.

"When you finish an orange, you don't feel like you need another one."

"You don't after some good pussy, either; you just feel good, and relaxed."

"At first, but eventually you need it again. And an orange doesn't have that tension while you're eating it," the first said, chewing two slices at once. "Want some?" he offered a piece to the other boy.

"Sure," said the second, taking the large chunk. He bit into it, carefully pulling the half in his hand away from his mouth. The two ate in silence for a moment. Chatter could be heard from across the field.

Swallowing, the second said, "Oranges squirt all over your clothes, if you're not careful."

"No comment."

Each took another bite. "Oranges don't play with your mind," said the first.

"Yeah. I dunno." The second shrugged his shoulders again. "Can I have another piece?"

Benjamin D. Martin, age 18

ME AND WOMAN KIND

How unfair,
you with your unpronounced,
unrecognized power.
Smooth sexy hips are your Gestapo,
erotic eyes your surveillance cameras.
The words you speak are more powerful,
more controlling than Big Brother.
Caught in the tangle of your hair,
I convince myself
I AM disloyal, I AM independent,
I control my freedom.
You, teenage queen, don't
own what I think,
nor lease my opinions.
But,
like a faithful pup,
I bound back,
sniffing for love,
competing for attention, distraction,
meaning.

Samuel Fox, age 17

———

a kiss

on

the

back of

the

neck

lying

next to

her

he

has felt her

breath

on his

neck; the soft

hairs

bristling

she stands and he lunges

to   grab   her

hand but

she

is

gone like every

thing else

and he

sits on

his bed

alone

Scott Baker, age 17

"So what's up between us? I don't want to call you my girlfriend. I don't want to call you anything. I don't want to mix you up with any fixed idea, with something that ought to be true. What am I scared of? I'm scared of being loved. Letting somebody love me, letting my guard down, showing you everything. I just want you to be there. Okay, so that's what I want. I'll see you again, right?"

Thomas Andrade, age 18

"JULIA"

What did we have?
    We had some pretty good times.
    and some great conversations
    about politics and the meaning of life
    and
    GOD
    (in all capital letters)
    although we never once discussed
    emotions.
    (But lord could you make me laugh.
    Like a downpour.)

And I ended it all
    Because of a cheap two-bit
    SLUT
    (In all capital letters)
    who liked to make me feel overly important
    and hated your guts
    for some reason
    until she won.

I miss you.

Todd VanDerWerff, age 18

"DANA"

Whatever love I have for you
is so rational that
I want there to be a car chase
or a wacky misunderstanding
or *some*thing
like where you turn out to be
        my long lost cousin
because the fact that everything
is going so gosh-darned flippin' expletive-deleted perfectly
just drives me *crazy*.
We seem dictated by the sitcom gods.

And yet there is a passion
in the way you grab my arm
or the way you wave good-bye to me as you drift away
that makes me want to wait around
to see what's there.

Todd VanDerWerff, age 18

OF EARTHWORMS AND YOU

sun's misplaced in the universe
galaxies fade
and planets disperse
every day is dark and drab
find my pleasure in
science lab
gone from the hope of your embrace
i stop and find
myself emasculate
dissect an earthworm
with a knife
and strike a point for
animal rights
saggy ascus and liverworts
i'd buy you back
but i'm afraid
iwishiwere
Omniscient
(don't ask me what it means)
sweatsocks and urine overpower me
as i walk into the rancid heat
you fell for gelboy and his hair
davy crockett shot a bear
i loved you and you loved me
gymnosperms grow inch by inch

(i suppose you wanted atticus finch
after all, gregory pecks a
hottie i guess)
disjointed ramblings
from a twisted brain
are all i have to hide the pain.
in a perfect world
x always equals three
if memphis is in tennessee
overwhelm me with self-pity
as mormons move to salt lake city
(i was never very good at history
but i'm worse without you)
give gelboy all my best
as for me I remain
Obsessed.

Todd VanDerWerff, age 16

Sort of a fly
On a pair of jeans
Without a zipper.
That's you.
Sort of a slit
In a wrist that's
Been roughly gashed.
That's you.
Sort of two lips
Without a mouth
To hold cigarettes
And talk.
That's you, in a way.

Ward Hoelscher, age 17

———————

An easy clean-up
on the cold linoleum floor
after igniting my spark
on the bathroom's cool squares.
All it takes
is a Kleenex
to roll away my passion
and headstrong lust.
I feel empty.
Have I betrayed
God or
just myself?

Todd VanDerWerff, age 17

GUTS

With her he had some classes
And saw her every day.
His eyes always seemed to wander
Towards her general way.
Quite the crush had developed;
Within love he was enveloped.
He could have asked her right away,
But didn't have the guts.

If she peered a little left
And tilted her head correctly,
She could face the teacher, yet
Still watch him indirectly.
He was ever a distraction;
She couldn't even do subtraction.
All but three words she could say;
She didn't have the guts.

Just a single moment needed,
Yet many a moment passed.
While unrequited love grew deeper,
Quickly the years elapsed.

They thought their fears to be a crime
And made me write this sappy rhyme,
To warn you all this very day:
You'd better have the guts.

Kevin N. Gabayan, age 17

MAIL

Tomorrow I'm going to
seal up my heart
and send it to
my one true love.
When she receives it,
I hope she will sign for it
and send me hers.

Emmanuel E. Carter, age 14

FLOATING

—FOR ADRIEN

White blossoms at our feet
we walked a small even trail of sunlight
our jackets shielding us from the wind
our hands tightly gripping our book bags.
Every day this trail led us through our mysterious city
the sound of cars zooming by, horns pounding,
the distant chatter of grade school children,
a symphony in the city.
The weather here was never cold—
her smile is what kept me warm,
though the sun remained lost in the sky
leaking orange light.
A shower kept us pure,
infants in the breath of innocence.
We always talked on our walk home from school,
our thoughts sailing on an ocean of clouds and stars.
In twenty years, she would be a nurse and I a doctor, or
in her version, she would be the president
and I the first man.

We floated our dreams on clouds
until she moved away—
the photograph torn in half.
Now I walk this cold trail alone,
pacing the concrete
without her light to keep me warm.

Stephan Johnson, age 18

I need to do something,
Write a letter,
Let it go somehow.
My heart attaches
To things, people.
When there is collision,
I lose myself in it,
In confusion.
Why not have two hearts?
I don't understand love,
But I know it exists.

Thomas Andrade, age 17

SONG FOR MY FATHER

Death is a sad song that embraces even children.
If I could have known my father, my heart would mourn.
I can only wish to talk to the sky and imagine
hearing his voice.
He left me his name but no name at all.
I would use my only father as a raft to float
through these rivers.
At night I say "I love you" and hear no response.
The song of his silence is thrown down from pulsating stars
telling me to go on.

Stephan Johnson, age 17

The entire course of my life was determined for me one muggy summer day in 1980 before I was even born. Everything I have in my life, I have because of a woman I have never met.

In twenty days, I will be able to find her.

The feeling is odd. I have anticipated this moment since the time my mother sat me down and told me about how I came to South Dakota because "there were some people who weren't able to take care of a baby, so they decided to give it to someone else."

I imagine the moment it all happened. The woman peers down at the tiny bundle softly sleeping, and leans in to kiss the child's forehead, knowing she'll never see him again. A nurse takes the baby away and the young woman in Michigan lies weeping in her hospital bed, preparing for the awful and inevitable task of getting on with her life.

Seven hundred miles away, in a hog-shed in southeastern South Dakota, a woman in overalls receives a phone call from an office in Michigan, informing her that "we have a late Christmas surprise for you and your husband." She leans on the wall, crying tears of joy and praising God, then rushes off to find her husband. The calls go out to every corner of the nation. Uncles in Ohio and aunts in North Carolina, great-aunts in California and grandparents in Huron and Armour. Grandma dives into her yarn pile to begin crocheting baby jumpers and socks and blankets and afghans.

And so, I came into the world. My mom has all the newspaper clippings. I was mentioned in the church news and in a few thank-you ads. The baby cards fill an entire hundred-page scrapbook. It seemed everyone was happy.

But I wonder about the young woman from Michigan. I wonder where she is and if she thinks about me anymore. If she wonders whether or not she made the right decision. There's a ring of fatalism to my life. What ifs plague me like phantom hounds. What if she had decided to keep me? What if she had chosen adoptive parents who lived in Florida instead of here? What if she had had an abortion? But something stopped her from getting one. And for that, I thank her a million times over, though my echoes of gratitude fly out into emptiness.

She was courageous, thoughtful, and compassionate in a way that few people are today. It is impossible for me to hate her, no matter HOW hard I try. I love her in spite of myself. She loved me. I know it. I have the files that tell her story and how she wept when she gave me up.

And how can I hate someone who sent me here? For all of my complaining, I have found everything someone could ever want out of life in this town. In my scant seventeen years on Earth, I have found loving family, caring friends, success, and the kinds of people I will be loath to leave when I go off to college. I've confronted death, hope, faith, God, my own future, and love on the streets and windswept prairies of this town and I thank her for that.

But the time draws near that I will be able to seek her out. And I am afraid. What if she doesn't want to see me? What if she doesn't live up to my expectations? What if she has died? I don't know if I'm ready for any of that. And when people say to me, well-meaningly, naturally, "Todd, are you going to find your birth parents?" I am forced to say, "I don't know." They are always shocked at my response, but they don't understand what it's like to be haunted by the ghost of a woman out of my past that I have never met or spoken to. When the day comes that I am ready to seek her out, I will know. And that day will come eventually. Her voice still calls to me loud and clear through the mists.

And somewhere in Michigan, a thirty-something woman washes the dishes, grades some papers, and fixes a little supper for her kids. She always gets a little restless in November and nobody really knows why. Maybe it's the onset of winter or maybe it's the leaves falling off of all the trees, but only her closest friends and family will ever know that it's really something else entirely. For she is haunted by her past. And the baby she loved too much to keep . . .

Todd VanDerWerff, age 17

TIME LOST FOREVER?

On Mondays, he'd try to help me out on homework.
But I'm so independent, I'd get mad.
He'd clean my room for me on days he was off from work
and I'd get angry 'cause my things were misplaced.
He'd joke around with me on days I didn't want
to be bothered. Now we are separated,
my homework is all wrong, and my room is a mess.
If I could go back, I'd listen and laugh, but I can't.
When I go over to his house, he won't help
with my homework. He doesn't laugh with me at my jokes.
Yesterday, though, he chuckled at something I said.
That was the first time in a long time. Perhaps it was
the re-beginning of something spectacular.

John H. Taylor, age 17

DEAR GOD

I want to live my life
through peace and knowledge.
I want to grow up
without fear.
I want to be like
my mother and father.
I want to have my
brothers and sisters care for me.
I want to be a good person
to everyone.
I want to be a good person
to myself.
I want to wake up
to clean, fresh air
blowing in my face.
I want to sit in front
of my fireplace
just waiting
to see
what's going to happen.

John Merrell, age 14

A POEM FOR US

What god was it that plucked us
from heaven's branches
sewed us into our mothers' wombs
to sprout
to blossom
to be beautiful for us?

What god was it that slid us onto this planet
as slick as we are
with lightning for tongues
and gave us the task of poets?

I don't concern myself with things too much to think of
it's all irrelevant now, because

we are nothing less than great
but that's too much to believe, isn't it?

always trying to ease out of these bodies
I too know despondency
like I know the rolling, shifting
uneasy feeling of my spirit

I know discontent, as much
as my eyes know to retreat,
peeling back from the sight of my reflection

we are nothing less than great
but this truth we dread, waving blazing fists in its face
clenching doubt in our tender palms
because we are too afraid to love ourselves

how have we managed to travel so little
yet hate ourselves so much
Ginsberg said he saw the best minds of his generation
destroyed
I have seen the same

I have seen us in our rooms
foils and lighters in our hands
straw in our lips and our noses
chasing black dragons and snorting white cobras
because 10 dollars was cheap
for a double hit of joy

I have seen us hunched over toilet bowls
vomiting self-esteem down the drain
because *Vogue* and *Elle* always
dressed beauty in a size 3 and that
was only a heave-ho and upchuck away

I have seen us on the corner
complacent and numb
copping doom in dime bags
because we didn't know that
the grim reaper wore Filas and a hoodie

I have seen us swigging
golden poison because we
were fooled and made to believe that manhood
could be sold in 40-ounce bottles

I have seen us spread our legs like the horizon
because some man tricked us into believing
that love could only be found on our backs

I have seen
us
I have seen
us

and I am not a coward anymore
I see us for what we are
nothing less than great, because
we are the poets

the derelict cats who prance on fine lines of chance
the sky rips open for us, luck lands on our laps
we confuse the wind, dismiss it

and send it off to all directions
we tap-dance on the shoulders of waves
and give height to the tides
we walk and talk mountains
breathe hurricanes, hum earthquakes
and our kisses are wet haikus glistening on crimson pages

we are nothing less than great
more than divine
but great and divine are still just words
words still have walls
walls are nothing but limits
but we are limitless beyond articulation

the world is waiting, holding its breath, waiting for us
the poems are waiting, holding their breath, waiting for us
they are waiting for us
to speak our thunder
to claim the mountaintops
to siphon the sun into our pens
and illuminate the page

just take my hand
time is flying away on precious gilded wings
we cannot be cowards anymore
the stakes are too high
the poems are too many

just take my hand
there's a universe for us to write about
and stars for us to conquer
let's start right here on this mountaintop
where we are gods and goddesses
who do not know the meaning of defeat
take my hand if you want
and let's write these poems together

Timothy Arevalo, age 19

The elements are at their peak.

Clouds raging, rain falling.

It's the kind of day that makes you think . . .

What does age bring, wisdom or confidence?

Will I ever know what I need to know?

Is there such a thing as an adult?

When I get there, if I get there . . . I won't forget.

Kyle Blanchard, age 16

A feeling,

    not necessarily of "I can."

    not even that "things will change."

    but undeniable courage

    to see the future through.

dr, age 18

Poems about love straight from teens

Falling Hard
100 Love Poems by Teens
edited by Betsy Franco

"The teen poets in this lively anthology knock
greeting-card clichés even as they celebrate their
romance and their passion and vent their hurt, anger,
and longing. . . . These poems will ring true." —*Booklist*

"Franco presents poets ranging in age from 13 to 18.
They are gay, lesbian, straight, transgender, and bisexual.
Most of the poets represent a diverse America, but some
are from other parts of the world. . . . Love, in all its raw,
uncensored intensity is here wonderfully captured
in verse by teen for teens." —*Kirkus Reviews*

Available in hardcover and paperback

www.candlewick.com